What Is Friction?

By Lisa Trumbauer

Consultants
David Larwa
National Science Consultant

Nanci R. Vargus, Ed.D.
Assistant Professor of Literacy
University of Indianapolis
Indianapolis, Indiana

Children's Press®
A Division of Scholastic Inc.
New York   Toronto   London   Auckland   Sydney
Mexico City   New Delhi   Hong Kong
Danbury, Connecticut

Designer: Herman Adler Design
Photo Researcher: Caroline Anderson
The photo on the cover shows children sledding in the snow.

Library of Congress Cataloging-in-Publication Data

Trumbauer, Lisa, 1963–
    What is friction? / by Lisa Trumbauer.
        p. cm. — (Rookie read-about science)
    Includes index.
    Summary: Describes what friction is and gives some examples of how it
    causes moving things to stop.
        ISBN 0-516-23447-1 (lib. bdg.)   0-516-25843-5 (pbk.)
        1. Friction—Juvenile literature. [1. Friction.] I. Title. II. Series.
    QC197.T78 2003
    531'.1134—dc22
                                                    2003019063

CHILDREN'S PRESS, and ROOKIE READ-ABOUT®,
and associated logos are trademarks and or registered trademarks
of Scholastic Library Publishing. SCHOLASTIC and associated logos
are trademarks and or registered trademarks of Scholastic Inc.

1 2 3 4 5 6 7 8 9 10 R 13 12 11 10 09 08 07 06 05 04

A race car zooms around a track. It is going very fast. How will it stop?

The driver steps on the brake pedal. This makes the brakes rub against the wheels.

The rubbing makes the wheels stop. This rubbing is called friction.

Friction is what stops things that are moving.

If there was no friction, things would keep moving forever.

Things do stop. That is how we know there is friction.

You cannot see friction, but you can see things that make friction.

Spin the wheel on a bike.
Now press the hand brake.

Watch closely.

The brake rubs against the
wheel. The brake makes
friction. The wheel stops.

brake

Friction happens because nothing is totally smooth. A street has lots of bumps.

Car tires have grooves.
The bumps and grooves
make friction.

Things that look very smooth have some friction, too.

Rubbing against water slows things down. That is why many fish are smooth.

They make less friction swimming in the water.

Things moving through the air also make friction.

The outside of airplanes are very smooth. The airplanes will make less friction as they rub against the air.

They will go faster.

The bottoms of your sneakers make friction. Your sneakers have grooves and bumps.

The grooves and bumps
stop you from sliding.

Basketball players need friction.

A basketball court has a smooth floor. The players' sneakers make friction.

This friction stops them from sliding on the smooth floor.

The more bumps
something has, the
more friction it makes.

A bumpy trail makes more friction than a smooth floor.

Roll a toy car across a smooth floor. It moves fast.

Does it keeping going?

No! Friction makes it stop.

Roll the same car on a carpet. It moves more slowly.

The carpet makes more friction. It has more bumps than the smooth floor.

On your mark.

Get set.

Go!

Friction will help you stop.

Words You Know

airplane

brake

grooves

smooth

sneakers

31

Index

About the Author

Lisa Trumbauer has written a dozen books about the physical sciences and dozens more about other branches of science. She has also edited science programs for teachers of young children. Lisa lives in New Jersey with one dog, two cats, and her husband, Dave.

Photo Credits

Photographs © 2004: Corbis Images: 6 (Reuters NewMedia Inc.), 16, 30 top (Royalty-Free), 3 (Mark L Stephenson); Ellen B. Senisi: 24, 27; Photo Researchers, NY: 5 (Bernard Asset), 13, 31 top (George Haling), 9 (Richard Hutchings); PhotoEdit: 28 (Michelle Bridwell), 19 (Tony Freeman), 18, 31 bottom right (Bonnie Kamin), cover (David Young-Wolff); Stone/Getty Images/Chuck Davis: 15; The Image Works: 23, 31 bottom left (Sonda Dawes), 20 (Jacksonville Journal Courier), 22 (Michael Okoniewski); Visuals Unlimited: 11, 30 bottom (Jeff J. Daly), 12, (Mark E. Gibson).